What peop

What is New Covenant Theology? An Introduction.

"This small book is a doctrinal pamphlet packed with straight-forward, palatable teaching on New Covenant Theology (NCT) distinctives regarding seven major Christ-centered doctrinal areas. It will surely provide a valuable service to those church members for whom it was intended, written by a gifted scholar. Although small, it is an important work that explains the essence and basis for a more accurate biblical and theological hermeneutical system. It is purposely designed in clear, succinct language to provide its target audience with what NCT is about in furtherance of the gospel. Pastors and teachers are encouraged to promote this fine, articulate work."

Gary D. Long,
Th.D., Faculty President, Providence Theological Seminary, Colorado Springs, CO

"Blake White has written a wonderfully accessible primer on New Covenant Theology. Some think the only options out there are Dispensationalism or Covenant Theology and have not even heard of New Covenant Theology. This is the ideal book to give to someone who wants a brief and convincing exposition of new covenant thought. I recommend this work gladly."

Thomas R. Schreiner,
James Buchanan Harrison Professor of
New Testament Interpretation,
The Southern Baptist Theological Seminary,
Louisville, Kentucky

"In a very readable, accurate, and succinct manner, Blake White covers the basics of New Covenant Theology. He nicely distinguishes NCT from Dispensational and Covenant Theology by showing NCT's distinctives, but in a way that is not complicated or difficult to understand. In addition, for those who often misunderstand NCT, this work also clearly teaches what is at the heart of NCT and how it seeks to understand the whole counsel of God in a way that is true to the Bible's own storyline and which is centered in Christ. I highly recommend this work for those who want to know more about NCT, for those who want to think through how "to put the Bible together," and mostly for those who want to rejoice in Jesus Christ our Lord, our glorious Mediator and Head of the new covenant."

Stephen J. Wellum,
Professor of Christian Theology,
The Southern Baptist Theological Seminary

"Blake White has given us another concise treatment on New Covenant Theology. His approach is "big brush strokes." This makes the work to be extremely useful for someone just becoming acquainted with New Covenant Theology. The author states his purpose at the beginning: 'In this book, I want to lay out the core concepts of New Covenant Theology … my aim is to make the essentials of New Covenant Theology available in an accessible way for church members.' I am sure the reader will quickly realize the author has attained his goal."

John G. Reisinger,
Evangelist and Author

"A. Blake White's book, *What is New Covenant Theology? An Introduction,* is exactly what it says! In clear, simple language White shows how this relatively new theological formulation tracks God's unfolding plan of redemption through the Bible to its culmination in Jesus Christ. All that God has done in Christ is truly amazing, and apprehending these truths opens up new vistas of adoration, understanding, and direction in living a life pleasing to God. If you want to better understand the Bible's own way of presenting the gospel, this book is highly recommended."

Kirk M. Wellum,
Principal, Toronto Baptist Seminary

"What attracts me to this way of seeing Scripture is its determination to use Bible words for Bible concepts, its commitment to following the progressive development of God's revelation, and its clear view of promise and fulfillment in the central figure of all revelation, Jesus Christ. I have friends and heroes on all sides of the discussion, but after years of Bible study on this subject, I have arrived where the author has arrived. I'm so thankful Blake White has put his studies into our hands and I recommend this book as a useful introductory guide to comprehending the aim of the Bible. I'll use it often."

Jim Elliff,
President, Christian Communicators Worldwide

"Blake White has done us a great service in making clear the basic ideas of New Covenant Theology. By reducing it to these basics it will make it easier to criticize and correct. So much controversy among Christians is due to not understanding the basic principles of the thing being argued about. For this reason I commend it to my fellow Christians. Also I commend it because I think it is right!"

Tom Wells,
Author of *The Christian and the Sabbath*,
The Priority of Jesus Christ, and many other books.
He is also co-author of *New Covenant Theology*.

"This book gets to the heart of the debate over New Covenant Theology. I commend the book for how concise and clear it is on key issues and I am especially excited by its irenic tone. May the Lord use it to move the discussion forward."

Jason C. Meyer,
Associate Professor of New Testament,
Bethlehem College and Seminary

"If you want a book that gets to the core of New Covenant Theology, this is it. When someone asks you to explain NCT, you now have a concise resource to put in their hands. Blake White has composed a helpful map for navigating the three major interpretive approaches to the Bible. Don't just read it, give copies to those who need to be reminded that Christ is all in all."

Douglas Goodin,
President,
Cross to Crown Ministries, Colorado Springs, CO

"Blake has given us a basic primer on New Covenant Theology that lays out the fundamental truths of this system of biblical truth. The book is easy to read and follow. The strength of the book is its clear explanation of the difference between the old covenant and the new covenant. This difference between the two covenants describes the essence of what New Covenant Theology is and why it is so different from Covenant Theology and Dispensationalism."

Geoff Volker,
Director of In-Depth Studies, Tempe, AZ

WHAT IS NEW COVENANT THEOLOGY?

AN INTRODUCTION

_____

A. Blake White

Other Books by A. Blake White:

The Newness of the New Covenant
The Law of Christ: A Theological Proposal
Galatians: A Theological Interpretation
*Abide in Him: A Theological Interpretation of
John's First Letter*
Union with Christ: Last Adam & Seed of Abraham

WHAT IS NEW COVENANT THEOLOGY?

AN INTRODUCTION

———————————

A. Blake White

5317 Wye Creek Drive, Frederick, MD 21703-6938
301-473-8781 | info@newcovenantmedia.com
www.NewCovenantMedia.com

What Is New Covenant Theology? An Introduction

Published by: New Covenant Media
             5317 Wye Creek Drive
             Frederick, MD 21703-6938
Cover design by: Matthew Tolbert

Printed in the United States of America

ISBN 13: 978-1-928965-44-2

To John G. Reisinger:

Standing on your shoulders, brother.
I am grateful for your faithfulness.

Table of Contents

Introduction

New Covenant Theology is a developing system of theology that seeks to let the Bible inform our theology. This sounds basic, and almost all systems of theology claim that their system is based upon the Bible. As I hope to show you, New Covenant Theology is the system of theology that allows the Bible to have the "final say" most consistently. Whereas Dispensationalism stands on presuppositions provided by its Scofield Bible and Covenant Theology stands on presuppositions provided by its Westminster Confession, New Covenant Theology does not have any outside document that must be imposed on the text of Scripture. It strives to let the sacred text speak on *its own terms*.

Currently there are three main systems of theology within evangelical Christianity which address the subject of redemptive history: Covenant Theology, Dispensationalism, and New Covenant Theology. Whether or not they are conscious of it, all Christians typically fall into one of these three systems (or perhaps some combination of them). Each system has its own way of relating the old covenant to the new covenant.

Generally speaking, Covenant Theology emphasizes continuity between the covenants to the expense of discontinuity. Since the Westminster Confession of Faith is structured around Covenant Theology, it is mostly Presbyterians who adhere to it, although others adhere closely to it as well (e.g., Reformed Baptists).

Dispensationalism, on the other hand, *tends* to emphasize discontinuity between the covenants at the expense of continuity. It is mostly Bible Churches that adhere to this system of theology, but it is certainly not limited to them. In America, Dispensationalism is by far the most popular of the three systems, due in large part to its adoption early on in the Fundamentalist movement, the hugely influential Scofield Reference Bible, radio and TV preachers, and popular marketing through fictional books and movies.

New Covenant Theology accommodates both continuity *and* discontinuity. It holds that the new covenant is connected to what went beforehand, but it is *new*. New Covenant Theology is held to by those in the "believer's church" tradition: those churches that emphasize believer's baptism and believe that the new covenant community consists of believers. The label "New Covenant Theology" is relatively new, but it is not a new method of interpretation. Several early church fathers, the Anabaptists, as well as other significant figures in church history "put the Bible together" in a similar way.

In this book, I want to lay out the core concepts of New Covenant Theology. There will be points where I sound like a Covenant Theologian, and points where I sound more like a Dispensationalist, but taken as a whole these essentials are uniquely New Covenant Theology. There are many more things that could be said, but *my aim is to make the essentials of New Covenant Theology available in an accessible way for church members.* Theological issues such as the millennium,[1] who the "all Israel" in Romans 11:26 refers to, whether or not there is a pre-fall covenant in Genesis 1-3, and the cessation or continuation of tongues and prophecy will not be addressed here. There is room for disagreement on these issues within New Covenant Theology.

So why is New Covenant Theology important? Why is it necessary? What's the big deal? *Jesus* is the big deal. Colossians 1:16 says that all things were created for Jesus. He is the center of the universe and the center of the Bible. Christ is the *pinnacle* of revelation. He is King! This has implications for his words. We must take *his* words with utmost seriousness. We interpret and apply every passage of Scripture in light of him. As 2 Corinthians 1:20 says, "For all the promises of God find their Yes in him. That is why it is through him that we utter our Amen to God for his glory." This will have unavoidable theological implications, and it seems to me that New Covenant Theology uniquely does justice to the authority and centrality of Jesus. I hope to show why in the following pages.

It is also important to wrestle with this theological issue because so many passages in the New Testament deal with the continuity and discontinuity between the old and new covenants. Just think of how many times the relationship between Jews and Gentiles is dealt with in the pages of the New Testament. Underlying those relational conflicts is the issue of how to interpret and apply the Old Testament in light of the coming of Jesus Christ.

Finally, I want to stress that this is an "in-house" discussion. At the end of the day, we are brothers and sisters united in Christ. The last thing we need in the church is arrogance and self-righteousness. We agree on the "big ones," the fundamentals of the faith. We must be properly balanced and keep the "main things" the main things. Where you land on this issue is not a test of orthodoxy. Having said that, I do think New Covenant Theology is the system of theology that is most consistent with the Protestant principle of *sola Scriptura* (Scripture alone), and am certain this discussion is one from which all Christians can benefit.

Chapter 1:
One Plan of God Centered in Jesus Christ

Jesus Christ is the center of all things! He is the center of redemptive history. All things point to him. As Colossians 1:16 puts it: "For by him all things were created, in heaven and on earth, visible and invisible, whether thrones or dominions or rulers or authorities—all things were created through him and for him." All the persons, events, and institutions of the Old Testament find their culmination in Christ. Jesus is the last Adam (Rom 5:12-21; 1 Cor 15:45), the second man (1 Cor 15:47), the true image of God (2 Cor 4:4), the seed of Abraham (Gal 3:16), the final sacrifice (Rom 3:25; John 1:29), the authoritative prophet like Moses (Deut 18:15; Acts 3:22), the Passover lamb (1 Cor 5:7), the one who brings about the new exodus (Luke 9:31), the inaugurator of a new and better covenant (Luke 22:20), the true tabernacle (John 1:14), the eternal priest after the order of Melchizedek (Heb 7), the end-time temple (John 2:19), the faithful son of David (Matt 1:1), the King anointed with the Spirit (Matt 3:16-17), and the suffering servant (1 Pet 2:24). God has one plan and that plan is centered upon Jesus the Messiah.

Covenant Theology agrees with New Covenant Theology that there is one plan of God, but they speak of this plan in terms of the "covenant of grace." This is a theological category used to show the presumed continuity between the covenants of Scripture. The problem is the Bible never uses such a term to describe God's plan. Instead, it uses the words "plan" and "purpose." The Bible also speaks of covenants (plural)[2] and not of a singular covenant.

The danger with using a theological category that is not found in Scripture is that we may eventually be compelled to distort the Scriptures themselves in order to accommodate it. A person can unintentionally end up twisting the Bible to make it say what fits with their system rather than letting the Bible inform and set the agenda *for* their system. In my opinion, this is exactly what the "covenant of grace" does. It tends to flatten out the old and new covenants, not doing justice to either covenant in its own biblical context. In order to maintain the man-made category of the "covenant of grace," Covenant theologians emphasize continuity within the plan of God even when there is discontinuity. We will see specific examples of this in chapter four.

New Covenant Theology strives to limit itself to using the language of the Bible. Ephesians 1:8-10 is a very important text for our system: "With all wisdom and understanding, he made known to us the mystery of his will according to his good pleasure, which he purposed in Christ, to be put into effect when the times reach their fulfillment—to bring unity to all things in heaven and on earth under Christ" (NIV). God has one will/purpose/plan, and it is to make Jesus central in all things. As we will see, there is both continuity and (radical) discontinuity within the one plan of God. I hope to show that God has a singular plan with multiple covenants, and that there is a sharp distinction between the old and new covenants.[3]

Some Dispensationalists teach that God has two plans: one for Israel and another for the church. The church is construed as a parenthesis in God's plan. Once the age of the church is over, God will pick his plan back up with Israel in a future millennium. God then, has two programs with two peoples. The essence of Dispensationalism is this distinction between Israel and the church.[4]

The story of the Bible is not the story of the covenant of grace; nor is it the story of Israel. The Bible is the story of God's work in history to sum up all things in Christ. New Covenant Theology strives to keep this one plan of God—centered in Jesus Christ—primary.

Chapter 2:
The Old Testament Should Be Interpreted in Light of the New Testament

We learn how to interpret the Old Testament from Jesus and his apostles. In many ways, this is the most important distinctive of New Covenant Theology. Hebrews 1:1-2 says, "Long ago, at many times and in many ways, God spoke to our fathers by the prophets, but in these last days he has spoken to us by his Son, whom he appointed the heir of all things, through whom also he created the world." God has revealed himself over time (progressively) and his revelation has come to a climax in Jesus Christ. Now all previous revelation must be understood in light of his centrality. Luke records that Jesus began with Moses and *all* the prophets and the Psalms, interpreting to his Emmaus followers the things concerning himself (Luke 24:27, 44). In John 5, Jesus told the Jews that the Scriptures bear witness about him (5:39). New covenant believers must approach the Old Testament with "Jesus lenses" firmly in place.

We must strive to read the Old Testament storyline in the same way the apostles did. God did not reveal himself all at once, but unfolded the Story over time. Revelation is progressive. History matters. We see the apostles taking note of the Old Testament narrative in a few key places in the New Testament. We won't take the time to explain the details of what is going on in each reference, but note the time indicators given to us: In Galatians 3, Paul points out the importance of realizing that the law came 430 years *after* the promise made to Abraham (Gal 3:17). The law was added *until* the Messiah should come (Gal 3:19). In Romans 4, the Apostle points out that Abraham was counted righteous *before* he was circumcised. He writes, "It was not after, but before he was circumcised" (Rom 4:10). The progression of the Story is very important for Paul's argument in these two chapters.

The author of Hebrews also reads the Bible *chronologically*. In Hebrews 3-4, he points out the significance of the fact that Psalm 95 speaks of "today" while rest was given to Joshua way back in Numbers. He writes, "For if Joshua had given them rest, God would not have spoken of another day *later on*" (Heb 4:8 emphasis mine). It is important for the point that the author of Hebrews is making that Psalm 95 comes, in his words, "so long afterward" (Heb 4:7), than Numbers in the storyline. The author of Hebrews makes a similar point in chapter 7 referring to the mention of Melchizedek in Genesis 14 and Psalm 110. In Hebrews 7:28 we read, "For the law appoints men in their weakness as high priests, but the word of the oath [that is, Psalm 110] which *came later* than the law, appoints a Son who has been made perfect forever." The mention of Melchizedek in Psalm 110 comes *after* the mention in Genesis 14. The apostles realized that God revealed himself over time. New Covenant Theology strives to follow their interpretive method.

Some Dispensational interpretations of the Old Testament are at odds with the interpretations of the apostles. When that happens, one should quickly go back to the drawing board. The apostles were moved along by the Holy Spirit (2 Pet 1:21) and are therefore authoritative guides. It will be helpful to take a look at several biblical examples.

Land Promises

How do the apostles understand the "land" promise to Israel? Do they envision the Jewish people being restored to Jerusalem? One looks in vain for such teaching in the New Testament. In Romans 4:13, Paul says that Abraham was promised the *world*! The text reads, "For the promise to Abraham and his offspring that he would be heir of the world." We should not brush this off, but should pause and ask what the Holy Spirit, through Paul, is teaching here. Paul is what we could call a *biblical theologian*. He interprets the Old Testament in light of Jesus. After his experience on the road to Damascus, nothing was the same for Paul. Now he reads Israel's Scriptures in light of the cross and resurrection. He sees everything in the Old Testament as *prophetic*, that is, pointing forward to Jesus and the new covenant he inaugurated.

So now, when Paul thinks about the "land" promise, he looks both backward and forward. The promise of land given to Abraham is rooted in God's original creation purposes. And, God's original creation purpose pointed to God's eventual new creation purpose. The original creation pointed forward to the new creation. Eden pointed forward to what God would eventually do: the *New* Eden. Jerusalem pointed forward to the *New* Jerusalem. Paul viewed the land as a *type* that pointed forward to the new creation, the whole world! The author of Hebrews agrees. He says that Abraham "was looking forward to the city that has foundations, whose designer and builder is God" (Heb 11:10). He was looking for Mount Zion, "the city of the living God, the heavenly Jerusalem" (Heb 12:22).

Does this mean that God did not keep his promise to Abraham? On the contrary—he elevated it immeasurably! Regarding the nature of the promise given to Abraham, Old Testament scholar Christopher Wright gives the following helpful illustration:

> Imagine a father who, in the days before mechanized transport, promises his son, aged 5, that when he is 21 he will give him a horse for himself. Meanwhile the motor car is invented. So on his 21st birthday the son awakes to find a motor car outside, "with love from Dad." It would be a strange son who would accuse his father of breaking his promise just because there was no horse. And even stranger if, in spite of having received the far superior motor car, the son insisted that the promise would only be fulfilled if a horse *also* materialized, since that was the literal promise. It is obvious that with the change in circumstances, unknown at the time the promise was made, the father has more than kept his promise. In fact he has done so in a way that *surpasses* the original words of the promise which were necessarily limited by the mode of transport available at that time. The promise was made in terms understood at the time. It was fulfilled in the light of new historical events.[5]

God will keep his promise to Abraham. Abraham and his children will have land. Indeed, they will ultimately inherit the whole world and reign with Christ forever.

The Gift of the Spirit

Strikingly, Paul also says that Abraham was promised the Holy Spirit. Galatians 3:14 says that Christ redeemed us "so that in Christ Jesus the blessing of Abraham might come to the Gentiles, so that we might receive the promised Spirit through faith." How can Paul say this? We don't read anything about the Holy Spirit in those chapters in Genesis, do we? Again, we must remember that Paul views all of the Old Testament in light of the new covenant. Paul was a *new covenant* theologian. He read the Abrahamic promises in light of the promises of the new covenant.

There are *two primary aspects* about the new covenant that make it *new*: (1) full and final forgiveness of sins and (2) the pouring out of the Holy Spirit upon all members of the covenant community. We will unpack this more later, but it is worth quoting two key prophetic passages here:

> Behold, the days are coming, declares the LORD, when I will make a new covenant with the house of Israel and the house of Judah, not like the covenant that I made with their fathers on the day when I took them by the hand to bring them out of the land of Egypt, my covenant that they broke, though I was their husband, declares the LORD. But this is the covenant that I will make with the house of Israel after those days, declares the LORD: I will put my law within them, and I will write it on their hearts. And I will be their God, and they shall be my people. And no longer shall each one teach his neighbor and each his brother, saying, 'Know the LORD,' for they shall all know me, from the least of them to the greatest, declares the LORD. For I will forgive their iniquity, and I will remember their sin no more. (Jer 31:31-34)

> I will sprinkle clean water on you, and you shall be clean from all your uncleannesses, and from all your idols I will cleanse you. And I will give you a new heart, and a new spirit I will put within you. And I will remove the heart of stone from your flesh and give you a

heart of flesh. And I will put my Spirit within you, and cause you to walk in my statutes and be careful to obey my rules. (Ezek 36:25-27)

Paul reads the promises made to Abraham through the lens of the great new covenant promises of Jeremiah 31 and Ezekiel 36. The Abrahamic covenant will find its ultimate fulfillment in the new covenant. This is the only way to make sense of what Paul says in Galatians 3:14 when he says that the blessing promised to Abraham included the gift of the Spirit. This is why he can also write, "Know then that it is those of faith who are the sons of Abraham. And the Scripture, foreseeing that God would justify the Gentiles by faith, preached the gospel beforehand to Abraham, saying, 'In you shall all the nations be blessed.' So then, those who are of faith are blessed along with Abraham, the man of faith" (Gal 3:7-9). Here Paul says that part of the blessing to the nations was justification (forgiveness of sins). All nations are blessed through Abraham by being justified by faith. Because Paul has the whole Old Testament in mind, he can see the blessings of the Abrahamic covenant as including the forgiveness of sins (i.e., justification) promised by Jeremiah and the gift of the Spirit promised by Ezekiel.

The True Offspring of Abraham

In Galatians 3:16, Paul continues his Christ-centered interpretation. There he writes, "Now the promises were made to Abraham and to his offspring. It does not say, 'And to offsprings,' referring to many, but referring to one, 'And to your offspring,' who is Christ." The promises given to Abraham were for him and Jesus. Jesus is the ultimate seed of Abraham. He is the true Israelite. Again, Paul sees the whole Old Testament finding its climax in Jesus. Faithful Jews were looking for this singular seed to come and defeat evil. Genesis 3:15 promised that the seed of the woman would crush the head of the serpent. This sets up the plotline of the Bible. Who will this seed be? As we saw, Abraham was promised offspring through whom all the nations would be blessed (Gen 12:1-3). Genesis 49:10 tells us that the scepter will not depart from the tribe of Judah and that the obedience of the nations will be his. So we see that this seed will come from the tribe of Judah. Moving further along the storyline, we see that God tells David that he will raise up his seed (or offspring) and will establish his kingdom forever (2 Samuel 7:12-13). This promised seed will be a son of David. Moving forward in the storyline once more, what does the first verse of our New Testaments begin with? Matthew 1:1: "The book of the genealogy of Jesus Christ, the son of David, the son of Abraham." Paul and Matthew read the promises to Abraham's seed in light of the whole Story of Scripture.

Consider several more examples where the New Testament quotes the Old Testament:

Joel 2:28-32

And it shall come to pass afterward, that I will pour out my Spirit on all flesh; your sons and your daughters shall prophesy, your old men shall dream dreams, and your young men shall see visions. Even on the male and female servants in those days I will pour out my Spirit. "And I will show wonders in the heavens and on the earth, blood and fire and columns of smoke. The sun shall be turned to darkness, and the moon to blood, before the great and awesome day of the LORD comes. And it shall come to pass that everyone who calls on the name of the LORD shall be saved. For in Mount Zion and in

Jerusalem there shall be those who escape, as the LORD has said, and among the survivors shall be those whom the LORD calls.

If we only had Joel and the other books of the Old Testament, it would be reasonable to conclude that Judah needs to turn to the Lord in order to be physically delivered on the day of the Lord. In other words, Judah would gain national and political freedom. These wonders in the heavens do not appear to have happened yet so it would also be reasonable to conclude that this must be pointing forward to a future day. Thankfully, we do not simply have the Old Testament. We have inspired apostles who give commentary on Joel's promise. In Acts 2:14-21, we find Peter interpreting Joel's prophecy in his Pentecost sermon. He states:

But Peter, standing with the eleven, lifted up his voice and addressed them: "Men of Judea and all who dwell in Jerusalem, let this be known to you, and give ear to my words. For these people are not drunk, as you suppose, since it is only the third hour of the day. But this is what was uttered through the prophet Joel: 'And in the last days it shall be, God declares, that I will pour out my Spirit on all flesh, and your sons and your daughters shall prophesy, and your young men shall see visions, and your old men shall dream dreams; even on my male servants and female servants in those days I will pour out my Spirit, and they shall prophesy. And I will show wonders in the heavens above and signs on the earth below, blood, and fire, and vapor of smoke; the sun shall be turned to darkness and the moon to blood, before the day of the Lord comes, the great and magnificent day. And it shall come to pass that everyone who calls upon the name of the Lord shall be saved'."

Peter says that "This is what was spoken by the prophet Joel." Will we listen to Peter? Will we follow his God-breathed interpretation of Joel (2 Tim 3:16)? Peter says that Joel's prophecy is fulfilled in the Spirit being poured out on

Jews and Gentiles. Peter says that all—regardless of ethnicity—who call upon the name of the Lord will be saved. Was Peter talking about physical deliverance from a locust plague? No, he was referring to the forgiveness of sins for both Jews and Gentiles (Acts 2:38)! We should take his interpretation *literally*.

Not surprisingly, Paul agrees with Peter. In Romans 10:12-13, he quotes Joel 2:32: "For there is no distinction between Jew and Greek; for the same Lord is Lord of all, bestowing his riches on all who call on him. For 'everyone who calls on the name of the Lord will be saved'." Again, Paul isn't referring to the physical deliverance of Judah, but the forgiveness of sins for Jew and Gentile alike.

Amos 9:11-12

"In that day I will raise up the booth of David that is fallen and repair its breaches, and raise up its ruins and rebuild it as in the days of old, that they may possess the remnant of Edom and all the nations who are called by my name," declares the LORD who does this. "Behold, the days are coming," declares the LORD, "when the plowman shall overtake the reaper and the treader of grapes him who sows the seed; the mountains shall drip sweet wine, and all the hills shall flow with it. I will restore the fortunes of my people Israel, and they shall rebuild the ruined cities and inhabit them; they shall plant vineyards and drink their wine, and they shall make gardens and eat their fruit."

If this were all we had, we might conclude that God planned to "literally" restore the nation of Israel on the day of the Lord. But remember, God's revelation of his plan unfolds *progressively*. James helps us out here. In Acts 15:16-18, he quotes Amos 9:11-12 to refer to the gathering of God's elect Jews *and* Gentiles. James notes that God has intervened and visited the Gentiles to "take from them a people for his name. And with this the words of the prophets agree." He then quotes Amos (Acts 15:14-18). Now, we must ask ourselves again: Will we go with James, or insist on our own interpretive approach? It seems most prudent to learn how to interpret the Old Testament from Jesus and his Spirit-led apostles.

Many more passages could be appealed to, but I hope with this sample I have shown how important it is to realize that God has revealed himself over time. Revelation is *progressive.* All previous Scripture must now be seen in light of Jesus and his apostles. The Father has told us who to listen to: His Beloved Son. Do you remember the story of the Transfiguration? It is fascinating. Moses was there, representing the law, and Elijah was there, representing the prophets. The Father says of Jesus, "This is my beloved Son, with whom I am well pleased; listen to him" (Matt 17:5). Then the disciples fell down to the ground in fear. Matthew tells us that when Jesus touched them, they looked up and "saw no one but Jesus only" (17:8). He is the key to interpreting the whole Bible!

Chapter 3:
The Old Covenant Was
Temporary by Divine Design

Another key distinctive of New Covenant Theology is that we believe the old covenant, as a whole, was temporary *by divine design*. God *meant* for it to be an interim covenant, a parenthesis in redemptive history. This is another way of saying that the new covenant really is *new*. The New Testament is crystal clear that new covenant Christians are no longer under the law of Moses. Let's examine a number of clarifying passages:

1 Corinthians 9:20-21 — *"To the Jews I became as a Jew, in order to win Jews. To those under the law I became as one under the law (though not being myself under the law) that I might win those under the law. To those outside the law I became as one outside the law (not being outside the law of God but under the law of Christ) that I might win those outside the law."*

Notice that Paul lays out three categories of people here:

- Those under the law (Jews)
- Those not having the law (Gentiles)
- Those who are not free from God's law but are under Christ's law (new covenant Christians)

Paul doesn't see himself as Jew or Gentile, but *Christian*. He is not under the law (the old covenant law of Moses), but neither is he without the law of God. He is not free from God's law but is "in-lawed to Christ" (*ennomos Christou*). Paul wants his hearers to know that, just because he is not under the Mosaic law, that does not mean he now lives however he wants. No, he is now under the jurisdiction of Jesus.

> **2 Corinthians 3:5-11** — *"Not that we are sufficient in ourselves to claim anything as coming from us, but our sufficiency is from God, who has made us competent to be ministers of a new covenant, not of the letter but of the Spirit. For the letter kills, but the Spirit gives life. Now if the ministry of death, carved in letters on stone, came with such glory that the Israelites could not gaze at Moses' face because of its glory, which was being brought to an end, will not the ministry of the Spirit have even more glory? For if there was glory in the ministry of condemnation, the ministry of righteousness must far exceed it in glory. Indeed, in this case, what once had glory has come to have no glory at all, because of the glory that surpasses it. For if what was being brought to an end came with glory, much more will what is permanent have glory."*

Here, Paul has some strikingly negative things to say about the old covenant. It kills. But the new covenant, because it includes the gift of the Spirit, gives life! Notice the way Paul compares the two covenants: the old kills, the new gives life; the old came with glory, the new is *more* glorious; the old is glorious, the new has *surpassing* glory; the old is transitory, the new is lasting!

> **Romans 6:14** — *"For sin will have no dominion over you, since you are not under law but under grace."*

This verse strikes the careful reader as a surprise. In the preceding verses of chapter 6, Paul has been talking about how those united to Christ have died to sin. After the first thirteen verses, we would expect Paul to say that we are no longer under sin, but under grace. The fact that he mentions the law is surprising at first glance. We must keep in mind that for Paul, the law is part of the old age, as we will see below. New covenant Christians are no longer under the old covenant era of law, but are now under the new covenant era of grace inaugurated by Christ himself.

Romans 7:4-6 — *"Likewise, my brothers, you also have died to the law through the body of Christ, so that you may belong to another, to him who has been raised from the dead, in order that we may bear fruit for God. For while we were living in the flesh, our sinful passions, aroused by the law, were at work in our members to bear fruit for death. But now we are released from the law, having died to that which held us captive, so that we serve in the new way of the Spirit and not in the old way of the written code."*

New covenant Christians are dead to the law (Gal 2:19). We are no longer bound to the law of Moses, but now "belong to another." This is very similar to what Paul said in 1 Corinthians 9:20-21. We are no longer under law but are "inlawed to the Messiah." We belong to him! We have been released from the old covenant law. Being bound by the written code — the law — was the old way. Now we serve God in the new way of the Spirit.

Galatians 3:23-25 — *"Now before faith came, we were held captive under the law, imprisoned until the coming faith would be revealed. So then, the law was our guardian until Christ came, in order that we might be justified by faith. But now that faith has come, we are no longer under a guardian,"*

Paul uses an important word here that we need to understand if we are going to grasp his point. He says that before the new age ("faith") came, Jews were held in custody. They were locked up. The law was their "guardian" (*paidagōgos*) until the Messiah brought about the new covenant. The word Paul uses for "guardian" would be better translated as "babysitter."[6] In the first century, the "guardian" was distinct from the "teacher" (*didaskalos*). The "guardian" was a household servant who looked after the child and made sure that he was fulfilling his responsibilities. One of the duties of the "guardian" was to bring the child to the "teacher." Once the child reached maturity, the "guardian" was no longer needed. Paul's point is that the "guardian" is temporary. The law was our "guardian" *until* the Messiah came (Gal 3:19, 23, 24; 4:2). Now that the Messiah has inaugurated the new age, we are no longer under the babysitter.

Hebrews 8:6-13— *"But as it is, Christ has obtained a ministry that is as much more excellent than the old as the covenant he mediates is better, since it is enacted on better promises. For if that first covenant had been faultless, there would have been no occasion to look for a second. For he finds fault with them when he says: "Behold, the days are coming, declares the Lord, when I will establish a new covenant with the house of Israel and with the house of Judah, not like the covenant that I made with their fathers on the day when I took them by the hand to bring them out of the land of Egypt. For they did not continue in my covenant, and so I showed no concern for them, declares the Lord. For this is the covenant that I will make with the house of Israel after those days, declares the Lord: I will put my laws into their minds, and write them on their hearts, and I will be their God, and they shall be my people. And they shall not teach, each one his neighbor and each one his brother, saying, 'Know the Lord,' for they shall all know me, from the least of them to the greatest. For I will be merciful toward their iniquities, and I will remember their sins no more. In speaking of a new covenant, he makes the first one obsolete. And what is becoming obsolete and growing old is ready to vanish away."*

This passage contains the longest Old Testament quotation that appears in the New Testament. It is clear that the new covenant will replace the old covenant. It is also clear that the author of Hebrews sees this new covenant as having been established in the first century. It is clearly the church who receives the benefits of the new covenant.

Some Covenant theologians view the new covenant as a *renewed* covenant. To keep their theological system of continuity intact, they say that all of the covenants are simply new administrations of the same old covenant of grace given in Genesis 3.[7] But if we let the Bible set the agenda, we will *have* to conclude that the new covenant is not simply renewed. It is radically *new*. The Holy Spirit, through Jeremiah, says that this new covenant *will not be like* the old covenant (Jer 31:32).[8]

Old Age/New Age

From the New Testament perspective, history can be structured around two ages: the present age and the age to come (Matt 12:32; Luke 18:30; Eph 1:21; Gal 1:4). Jewish people before Christ thought that the Messiah would come and usher in the age to come. This age would be characterized by full forgiveness (Jer 31), the universal outpouring of the Spirit (Joel 2; Isa 32, 44), and resurrection (Dan 12:2; Ezek 37). What they did not expect was for one man to be raised in the middle of history. They did not realize that the Messiah would come in the middle of history and usher in the age to come *in the midst of* the present evil age. Commencing with the death and resurrection of the Messiah and the pouring out of the Spirit, the new age has dawned. In 1 Corinthians 10:11, Paul writes, "Now these things happened to them as an example, but they were written down for our instruction, on whom the end of the ages has come." Through Christ and the Spirit, God's future has invaded the present. Through the cross and resurrection, Jesus rescued his people from the present evil age (Gal 1:4).

This two-age structure is foundational for understanding most of the New Testament. This is the underpinning for all the contrasts in Paul's writings: flesh/Spirit, letter/Spirit, Adam/Last Adam, law/grace, sin/righteousness, law/faith, slavery/freedom, death/resurrection, law/gospel, futility/hope, decay/renewal, wrath/adoption, etc.[9] From Paul's perspective, the old covenant law is on the old age side of the old age/new age equation. Adam, law, and flesh are *old*, while Last Adam, Spirit, and righteousness are *new*. As previously noted, this is how Paul can say in Romans 6:14 that we are no longer under law but are now under grace. He could have just as easily have said that we are no longer in the old age, but are now in the new.

This was the major problem Paul was addressing in the letter to the Galatians. The Judaizers needed new "watch batteries;" they were confused over what time it was in God's plan. To use Anabaptist leader Pilgram Marpeck's terms, they were confusing yesterday with today.[10] That's why Paul begins and ends the Galatians letter the way he does. He opens the letter in 1:4 by saying Jesus has rescued us from the *present evil age* (he could have said old creation) and closes by mentioning the *new creation* (he could have said new age) in 6:15. The law is part of the old age. Praise be to Christ! We are no longer under the law. Or, as Philip Bliss put it in his classic hymn: "Free from the law, oh happy condition!"

Chapter 4:
The Law is a Unit

Another essential aspect of New Covenant Theology is its view that the old covenant law is a unit. It is a package deal. Another way to state this is to say that the law is bound up with the covenant in which it was given. One cannot separate the commands from the covenant to which they belong.

Following John Calvin, who followed Thomas Aquinas, Covenant Theology famously divides the law up into three categories, historically called the tripartite division of the law: moral, ceremonial, and civil. Depending on which type of Covenant Theology you are talking about, most will say that the ceremonial and civil aspects of the law have been abolished with the coming of Christ, but that new covenant Christians are still bound by the moral aspects of the law. According to this viewpoint, the moral law is summarized in the Ten Commandments (the Decalogue).

While we agree that *some* verses *can* be safely classified as moral, ceremonial, or civil, we find it unhelpful, and more importantly, unbiblical, to do so. One looks in vain for any biblical evidence for these classifications. Furthermore, *all* that God commands is *moral*, in the sense that it would have been immoral for an Israelite to disobey *any* command of God regardless of its "classification." Jews and first century Christians viewed the old covenant law as a unit. Here, again, we have to be careful to let the text itself drive the agenda. We want to get our theology *from* the text; not impose our theology onto the text. With their three-fold division of the law, we believe that advocates of Covenant Theology have imposed a man-made grid onto the text of Scripture to make it fit their theological system.

If our theological presuppositions are left behind, we will see from Scripture that the law is a unit. In Galatians 5:3, Paul wrote, "I testify again to every man who accepts circumcision that he is obligated to keep the *whole* law" (emphasis added). James 2:10 reads, "For whoever keeps the whole law but fails in one point has become accountable for *all of it*" (emphasis added). Hebrews 7:11-12 is very important for this point. The author writes, "If perfection could have been attained through the Levitical priesthood—and indeed the law given to the people established that priesthood—why was there still need for another priest to come, one in the order of Melchizedek, not in the order of Aaron? For when the priesthood is changed, the law must be changed also." The writer of Hebrews views the law as a package as well. He said that the law established the priesthood. The two are inseparable. He is making the case that the priesthood has changed with the coming of Christ, and "when the priesthood is changed, the law must be changed also" (NIV).[11] New Covenant theologians are not making up their theology, but are seeking to let the Bible inform their theology. The writer of Hebrews says that the law must be changed in the new covenant.

We also learn that the law and the covenant are a package from the giving of the law itself. First, let's consider the structure of the law in Exodus:

- Exodus 19—Historical Introduction
- Exodus 20—The Ten Words (what we know as the Ten Commandments)

- Exodus 21-23—The Rules
- Exodus 24—The Covenant Ceremony

Exodus 20:1 introduces the ten "words" and then lays out what we now call the Ten Commandments. Then, in Exodus 21:1, Moses begins to lay out the "rules" in chapters 21-23. So we have the historical introduction, the words, the rules, and then the covenant ceremony. What is important for our purposes is how Moses speaks of what we now know as these "chapters." Recall that Moses did not have the chapter breaks. Exodus 24:3 says, "Moses came and told the people all the words of the LORD and all the rules. And all the people answered with one voice and said, 'All the words that the LORD has spoken we will do'." Notice what the Bible says here. Moses told the people all the Lord's *words and rules.* For us, this means all of chapter 20 and chapters 21-23. Then, a few verses later, these words *and* laws are called "The Book of the Covenant" (Exod 24:7). The Book of the Covenant consists of the ten words *and the rules.* They all belong together. The law goes with the covenant. It is all one unit.

Chapter 5:
Christians are not Under the Law of Moses, but the 'Law' of Christ

We have seen that the people of God are no longer bound to the old covenant law of Moses. Covenant theologians say that believers are no longer bound to the civil and ceremonial parts of the law, but are still bound to the moral law, which for them is summed up in the Ten Commandments. As we have seen, one cannot pull the Ten Commandments out of the covenant and make them eternal moral law, transcending the covenant in which they were given. Furthermore, the New Testament clearly teaches that we are no longer bound to the Sabbath Commandment, which is the fourth of the Ten Commandments. If Paul thought that new covenant Christians were still bound to obey the Sabbath, do you think he would have ever said: "One person esteems one day as better than another, while another esteems all days alike. Each one should be fully convinced in his own mind" (Rom 14:5). Paul is a Sabbath relativist! He says to make up your own mind regarding the matter. This is a far cry from "Remember the Sabbath Day to keep it holy" (Exod 20:8). Do you remember the man who was stoned for gathering wood on the Sabbath? Clearly times have changed in the new covenant.

In Colossians 2:16-17, he wrote, "Therefore let no one pass judgment on you in questions of food and drink, or with regard to a festival or a new moon or a Sabbath. These are a shadow of the things to come, but the substance belongs to Christ." Christ has come! The reality is here. We are no longer slaves to the elemental spirits of the world—which includes observing the Sabbath (Gal 4:8-11)! The Sabbath pointed forward to the salvation rest we now find in Christ (see Heb 3-4). Interestingly, the word Paul uses in Colossians 2 for shadow (*skia*) is used by the author of Hebrews when he writes, "the law has but a shadow of the good things to come" (10:1).

If Christians are not bound to the law of Moses, are we free to live however we want? Doesn't this view produce worldly living since "God's law" is not there to keep us in check? As Paul would say, "By no means!" If anything, New Covenant Theology ratchets up the call for righteous living. Consider the many statements of Jesus in the Sermon on the Mount: You have heard it said in the Mosaic law that you shouldn't murder, *but I say to you* that if you are even angry with a brother or sister then you will be subject to judgment (Matt 5:21-22); You have heard it said in the law that you shouldn't commit adultery, *but I say to you* that if you so much as look at a woman lustfully you have already committed adultery in your heart (Matt 5:27-28).

Furthermore, we *are* under "God's law." The question is "What does God's law consist of in the new covenant?" First Corinthians 9:20-21 helps us answer this question. I used to say that this one verse was the reason I held to New Covenant Theology because, in my opinion, New Covenant Theology can uniquely do justice to this passage, but now I find myself saying the same thing about several passages of Scripture. The passage reads:

> To the Jews I became as a Jew, in order to win Jews. To those under the law I became as one under the law (though not being myself under the law) that I might win those under the law. To those outside the law I became as one outside the law (not being outside the law of God but under the law of Christ) that I might win those outside the law.

As noted above, there are three groups of people here: those under law (Jews), those without the law (Gentiles), and those under God's law (Christians). Paul clearly sees himself in the third position. He is a Christian; one who is bound to God's law by being "in-lawed to Christ" (*ennomos Christou*). Christians are not under the old covenant law of Moses, but to be "law-less" doesn't mean we are now lawless because we are now under the new covenant law of Christ. We learn the same truth a few chapters earlier in 1 Corinthians 7:19: "For neither circumcision counts for anything nor uncircumcision, but keeping the commandments of God." Clearly we are not under the law of Moses because the law of Moses commanded circumcision! Here Paul says that circumcision doesn't matter. All that matters is keeping God's commands. Since God's commands no longer include circumcision, Paul must be referring to the law of Christ, as he does a couple of chapters later in 1 Corinthians 9.

So we are not under the Mosaic law, but that doesn't mean we are now lawless. No, we are still bound to God's law—which now means being bound to Jesus (in-lawed to Christ). We now "belong to another" (Rom 7:4). We look to

Jesus our King. He shows us how to live in a way that pleases God.

Paul uses similar language in Galatians 6:2. There he says, "Bear one another's burdens, and so fulfill the law of Christ." What does Paul mean by "the law of Christ" or literally "the law of the Messiah" (*ton nomon tou Christou*)? There are really two main options: it is either the law of Moses or something different. Virtually all of the 30 preceding uses of "law" (*nomos*) in Galatians refer to the Mosaic law. This being the case, we must have good reason to say this is *not* a reference to the Mosaic law, and we do; here are three reasons:

First, there are so many negative references to the law in the first five chapters of Galatians:

2:16—*"a person is not justified by works of the law ... in order to be justified by faith in Christ and not by works of the law, because by works of the law no one will be justified."*

2:19—*"For through the law I died to the law"*

2:21—*"if righteousness were through the law, then Christ died for no purpose."*

3:2—*"Did you receive the Spirit by works of the law or by hearing with faith?"*

3:10—*"For all who rely on works of the law are under a curse;"*

3:11—*"Now it is evident that no one is justified before God by the law"*

3:12—*"But the law is not of faith"*

3:13—*"Christ redeemed us from the curse of the law"*

3:18—*"For if the inheritance comes by the law, it no longer comes by promise;"*

3:21b—*"If a law had been given that could give life, then righteousness would indeed be by the law."*

3:23—"Now before faith came, we were held captive under the law, imprisoned until the coming faith would be revealed."

3:24—"So then, the law was our guardian until Christ came,"

4:5—God sent his Son "to redeem those who were under the law,"

5:4—"You are severed from Christ, you who would be justified by the law;"

5:18—"But if you are led by the Spirit, you are not under the law."

5:23—"Against such things [the fruit of the Spirit] there is no law."

Prior to Galatians chapter 6, Christ and the law have been presented as being in sharp opposition. Only in Galatians 6:2 are the two used together positively. This fact suggests that Paul has some *other* "law" in mind here.

Second, Paul adds two extremely important words to the word *law: "of Christ"* (*tou Christou*)! Paul has in mind something distinct from the law of Moses here. He is thinking of a different law: the law of Christ.

Third, we saw in 1 Corinthians 9:19-21 that the law of Christ is something distinct from the law of Moses. Recall that there Paul clearly distinguishes the law of Moses from the law of God. Then he defines the law of God as being "inlawed to Christ" (*ennomos Christou*). In other words, one fulfills the will of God not by putting oneself under the law of Moses, but by being under the jurisdiction of Jesus.

These three points lead me to believe Paul has something different in mind for "law" in Galatians 6:2. But what exactly is it? I suggest that he is using an ironic, rhetorical word-play here, like he does with faith "working" in Galatians 5:6: "For in Christ Jesus neither circumcision nor uncircumcision counts for anything, but only faith working through love."[12] Throughout the letter Paul has also *contrasted* faith and works, but then towards the end he says that all that matters is faith "working." Paul is very clever. This is not the only time that Paul has used the word "law" metaphorically. Consider the following instances:

> Galatians 5:23 — *"Against such things [the fruit of the Spirit] there is no law."*

> Romans 3:27 — *"Then what becomes of our boasting? It is excluded. By what kind of law? By a law of works? No, but by the law of faith."*

> Romans 7:23 — *"But I see in my members another law waging war against the law of my mind and making me captive to the law of sin that dwells in my members."*

> Romans 7:25 — *"So then, I myself serve the law of God with my mind, but with my flesh I serve the law of sin."*

> Romans 8:2 — *"For the law of the Spirit of life has set you free in Christ Jesus from the law of sin and death."*

It is true that Paul usually has the Mosaic law-covenant in mind when he uses the word *law* (*nomos*) — but not always. The Galatians want to be under "law" so Paul grants it. In Galatians 6:2, Paul cleverly coins the phrase "law of Christ" to refer to the pattern of Christ. What is that "law" or "pattern"?

He has already shown what this pattern is in the letter to the Galatians. We are called to carry one another's burdens and in this way we will fulfill the "pattern" of Christ. Paul has presented Christ as the ultimate burden bearer. His readers would have already seen this in the letter:

Galatians 1:3-4—*"Grace to you and peace from God our Father and the Lord Jesus Christ, who gave himself for our sins to deliver us from the present evil age, according to the will of our God and Father,"*

Galatians 2:20—*"I have been crucified with Christ. It is no longer I who live, but Christ who lives in me. And the life I now live in the flesh I live by faith in the Son of God, who loved me and gave himself for me."*

Galatians 3:13-14—*"Christ redeemed us from the curse of the law by becoming a curse for us—for it is written, "Cursed is everyone who is hanged on a tree"—so that in Christ Jesus the blessing of Abraham might come to the Gentiles, so that we might receive the promised Spirit through faith."*

Galatians 4:4-5—*"But when the fullness of time had come, God sent forth his Son, born of woman, born under the law, to redeem those who were under the law, so that we might receive adoption as sons."*

Notice the pattern: Jesus gives of himself for the good of others. He gave himself so that we would be forgiven and delivered from this present evil age. He loved us by giving himself for us. He became a curse so that we would be redeemed from the curse and so that we would receive the promised Spirit. He was sent to redeem us so that we might receive adoption. He gave of himself for our good. This is his "law," his pattern.

So doing justice to the fact that Paul is using a word-play on the word "law" here in Galatians 6:2, a better translation may be "basic principle,"[13] or "regulative principle," or "structure of existence,"[14] or "normative pattern."[15] "Law" could also be translated as "main principle" since this burden-bearing, self-giving love is seen as the essence of what Christ was about. This is the "Torah" of the Messiah. It is his instruction. This is the "way of Jesus" (Rom 15:3, 7). This is the "Jesus mindset" (Phil 2:5).

It is a pattern of self-enslaving love. In Galatians 5:13, Paul exhorts us to become slaves of one another in love. Ironically, we use our freedom as an opportunity to become slaves of others. We are servants. We put the needs of others above our own. We give of ourselves for the good of others. This is the same thing Paul says in Philippians 2:3-8:

> Do nothing from rivalry or conceit, but in humility count others more significant than yourselves. Let each of you look not only to his own interests, but also to the interests of others. Have this mind among yourselves, which is yours in Christ Jesus, who, though he was in the form of God, did not count equality with God a thing to be grasped, but made himself nothing, taking the form of a servant, being born in the likeness of men. And being found in human form, he humbled himself by becoming obedient to the point of death, even death on a cross.

We are to give of self for the good of others. We put them first, just as Jesus put us first by becoming human and dying on a cross. He did not come to be served, but to serve.

New covenant Christians are not under the law of Moses but the law of Christ. This means that we are not primarily about law, but love! But from Galatians 5:14, we learn that this love *fulfills* the law. That verse reads, "For the whole law is fulfilled in one word: 'You shall love your neighbor as yourself'." That's precisely the teaching of Jesus: in Matthew 7:12 he said, "So whatever you wish that others would do to you, do also to them, for this is the Law and the Prophets." In Matthew 22:40, he said "On these two commandments [love of God and neighbor] depend all the Law and the

Prophets." Paul also teaches that love fulfills the law in Romans 13:10: "Therefore love is the fulfilling of the law." Through the Spirit and the cross, our love for one another brings to fruition what the law always pointed to and required.

This "cruciform" (cross-shaped) love is at the heart of new covenant ethics. One finds this call to love all over the New Testament. Consider a few of these passages and notice the pattern:

Ephesians 5:2 — *"And walk in love, as Christ loved us and gave himself up for us, a fragrant offering and sacrifice to God."*

2 Corinthians 8:9 — *"For you know the grace of our Lord Jesus Christ, that though he was rich, yet for your sake he became poor, so that you by his poverty might become rich."*

John 13:14-15 — *"If I then, your Lord and Teacher, have washed your feet, you also ought to wash one another's feet. For I have given you an example, that you also should do just as I have done to you."*

John 13:34 — *"A new commandment I give to you, that you love one another: just as I have loved you, you also are to love one another."*

Romans 15:2-3a — *"Let each of us please his neighbor for his good, to build him up. For Christ did not please himself,"*

1 Corinthians 10:32-11:1 — *"Give no offense to Jews or to Greeks or to the church of God, just as I try to please everyone in everything I do, not seeking my own advantage, but that of many, that they may be saved. Be imitators of me, as I am of Christ."*

It is clear that the heart of the law of Christ is cross-shaped love, but there is more to new covenant ethics than love. It also includes the teaching of Jesus and his apostles.

The law of Christ can be defined as those prescriptive principles drawn from the example and teaching of Jesus and his apostles (the central demand being love), which are meant to be worked out in specific situations by the guiding influence and empowerment of the Holy Spirit.[16]

Dispensationalism is similar to New Covenant Theology when it comes to new covenant ethics. Covenant Theology, on the other hand, can be described as being "law-centered." They would have us go to Christ for justification (our right standing with God) and to the law for sanctification (our growth in Christian maturity). New Covenant Theology can be described as "Spirit-driven and Christ-centered." The basic imperative of the new covenant is "walk by the Spirit" (Gal 5:16). There is great freedom in the new covenant. We are to be transformed by the renewal of the mind (Rom 12:1-2; cf. Phil 1:9-11; Col 1:9-10). This obviously does not imply that there are no external commandments needed. Far from it! Remember that in 1 Corinthians 7:19, Paul says that the only thing that counts is keeping God's commands. But we must see external commands as train tracks. They are needed to keep us in line, but they are different from the engine. The engine is the gospel of grace, the power of the Spirit, and the example of Jesus.

Chapter 6:
All Members of the New Covenant Community are Fully Forgiven and Have the Holy Spirit

Both Covenant Theology and Dispensationalism will agree with New Covenant Theology that all new covenant Christians are fully forgiven of their sins, so we don't have to spend much time on this point. It is the clear teaching of Jeremiah's new covenant promise: "For I will forgive their iniquity, and I will remember their sin no more" (Jer 31:34). Forgetting is passive, but "not remembering" is active. Praise God!

However, New Covenant Theology differs from Covenant Theology in how it understands Jeremiah when he says that in the new covenant community, "no longer shall each one teach his neighbor and each his brother, saying, 'Know the LORD,' for they shall all know me, from the least of them to the greatest, declares the LORD" (Jer 31:34). New Covenant Theology believes that *all* in the new covenant community *know* the Lord. All are *believers* in the new covenant community. Covenant Theology typically believes the new covenant community consists of believers and their unregenerate children.

Preceding his great new covenant promise, Jeremiah records the following proverb: "In those days they shall no longer say: 'The fathers have eaten sour grapes, and the children's teeth are set on edge.' But everyone shall die for his own sin. Each man who eats sour grapes, his teeth shall be set on edge" (Jer 31:29-30). Jeremiah is referring to the "tribal" nature of the old covenant.[17] Under the old covenant, the people's knowledge of God was largely dependent on special leaders. As the leaders went, so went the people.

The new covenant would not have this "tribal" structure. The entire covenantal structure will be replaced by a new one. The old covenant community was a "mixed" community, consisting of both genuine believers and unbelievers. The Spirit was only *selectively* and *temporarily* given in the old covenant, mostly on designated leaders (prophets, priests, and kings). For example, God calls Bezalel and fills him with his Spirit to enable him to help construct the tabernacle and all of its elements (Exod 31:2; 35:31; 36:1; cf. Hiram in 1 Kings 7:14). This is not to say that the Spirit of God never operated upon the old covenant remnant. God enabled the remnant of Israel to trust in his covenant promises, but they were not *indwelt* by the Spirit of God.

In the new covenant, however, *all* will know the Lord. As James Hamilton writes, "Under the new covenant, God would not have a tribe of priests ministering to the rest of His people, but His people as a whole would be a kingdom of priests (Exod 19:6; 1 Pet 2:9; Rev 1:6)."[18] Unlike the old covenant, *all* are indwelt by the Spirit in the new covenant. Moses longed for the day when all would have the gift of the Spirit. Numbers 11:29 says, "But Moses said to him, 'Are you jealous for my sake? Would that all the LORD's people were prophets, that the LORD would put his Spirit on them!'" The Old Testament Scriptures are replete with promises of a coming day where the Spirit-anointed King would pour out the Spirit in abundance. The new messianic age would be the age of the Spirit. Consider the following passages:

Ezekiel 11:19 — *"And I will give them one heart, and a new spirit I will put within them. I will remove the heart of stone from their flesh and give them a heart of flesh,"*

Ezekiel 36:25-27 — *"I will sprinkle clean water on you, and you shall be clean from all your uncleannesses, and from all your idols I will cleanse you. And I will give you a new heart, and a new spirit I will put within you. And I will remove the heart of stone from your flesh and give you a heart of flesh. And I will put my Spirit within you, and cause you to walk in my statutes and be careful to obey my rules."*

Isaiah 32:14-17 — *"For the palace is forsaken, the populous city deserted; the hill and the watchtower will become dens forever, a joy of wild donkeys, a pasture of flocks; until the Spirit is poured upon us from on high, and the wilderness becomes a fruitful field, and the fruitful field is deemed a forest. Then justice will dwell in the wilderness, and righteousness abide in the fruitful field. And the effect of righteousness will be peace, and the result of righteousness, quietness and trust forever."*

Isaiah 44:3 — *"For I will pour water on the thirsty land, and streams on the dry ground; I will pour my Spirit upon your offspring, and my blessing on your descendants."*

Joel 2:28-29 — *"And it shall come to pass afterward, that I will pour out my Spirit on all flesh; your sons and your daughters shall prophesy, your old men shall dream dreams, and your young men shall see visions. Even on the male and female servants in those days I will pour out my Spirit."*

These promises came to fruition at Pentecost, and not before then. The Spirit is the gift of the last days. Pentecost opened up a new stage in redemptive history. We know this from some important words in the gospel according to John. In John 7:39, John wrote "Now this he said about the Spirit, whom those who believed in him were to receive, for as yet the Spirit had not been given, because Jesus was not yet glorified." In John 14:17, Jesus says that we know the disciples know the Spirit, "for he dwells with you and will be in you." In John 15:26, Jesus says he will send (future tense) the Helper to the disciples. John 16:7 reads, "Nevertheless, I tell you the truth: it is to your advantage that I go away, for if I do not go away, the Helper will not come to you. But if I go, I will send him to you." These words are important and helpful. According to Jesus and John, the Spirit had not yet been poured out. The disciples were not yet indwelt by the Spirit. The indwelling of the Spirit did not come until Pentecost.

The new covenant was inaugurated with the life, death, and resurrection of Jesus, the pouring out of the Spirit at Pentecost, and the destruction of Jerusalem in AD 70. Jesus and the author of Hebrews apply the great new covenant promise of Jeremiah 31 to the church. Hebrews 8 quotes the promise in full and then adds: "In speaking of a new covenant, he makes the first one obsolete. And what is becoming obsolete and growing old is ready to vanish away" (8:13).

There are obvious implications for local church ministry from what we have said so far. Only *believers* in Jesus are to be baptized. The new covenant community consists only of those who are indwelt by the Spirit. The church is to be a *believer's* church. There is no biblical precedent for having a mixed community of believers and unbelievers in the new covenant church. All are fully forgiven and are indwelt by the Spirit of God.

Chapter 7:
The Church is the
Eschatological Israel

I know what you are saying, "The church is the eschat—a—what?" Eschatology is generally understood as the study of the end times (or last things), so when New Covenant Theology says that the church is the eschatological Israel, we are saying that the church is the end-time Israel. Dispensationalism teaches that the church and Israel are two separate peoples, while New Covenant Theology teaches that the church is the continuation of Israel through Jesus Christ. Sometimes, New Covenant Theology is accused of being "replacement theology," but this is unfair. New Covenant Theology does not teach that the church replaces Israel but that the church is the *fulfillment* of Israel by virtue of its union with the Jewish Messiah. As we have seen, *all* the promises of God are yes in Jesus Christ (2 Cor 1:20). It is not that Israel equals the church, as Covenant Theology teaches, but that Jesus is the climax and fulfillment of Israel and the church is the end-time Israel *because it is united to Jesus Christ, her covenant head.* New Covenant Theology is robustly Christ-centered. Jesus is the interpretive key to the relationship between Israel and the church. The covenant people of God have been reworked and redefined in light of the Messiah and the new covenant he inaugurated.

Dispensationalism insists that God must keep his promises to ethnic Israel, but what is often left unsaid is that God only made promises to *faithful* Israel—and there is only one wholly faithful Israelite: Jesus of Nazareth. He brings Israel's history to its intended climax. This is taught throughout the New Testament. The apostle Paul explicitly tells us that the seed of Abraham is *singular* (Gal 3:16). Matthew begins with the words: "The book of the genealogy of Jesus Christ, the son of David, the son of Abraham." In Matthew we have a Genesis: "The book of the genesis" (1:1 *biblos geneseōs*), an Exodus: "Out of Egypt I called my son" (2:15), a passing through the waters (3:13-17), desert temptations (4:1-11), a Deuteronomy in chapters 5-7 with Jesus giving his instruction (or "law") from the mount (5:1), followed by a royal and prophetic ministry, an exile (the cross), and finally the restoration (the resurrection of Jesus).[19] Jesus sums up Israel's history. It all pointed to him.

In the new covenant era, all who are united to the faithful Israelite are now themselves Israelites. The apostle Paul is crystal clear in this regard. Since the opponents addressed in the letter to the Galatians were teaching that Gentiles must live like Jews, Paul strives to show that Jew and Gentile are on equal ground now. Galatians 3:7 reads, "Know then that it is those of faith who are the sons of Abraham." The "sons of Abraham" is another way of referring to Israel. Paul says it is those of faith who are Israel. A few verses later in Galatians 3:16 we read, "Now the promises were made to Abraham and to his offspring. It does not say, 'And to offsprings,' referring to many, but referring to one, 'And to your offspring,' who is Christ." Jesus is the offspring of Abraham. In Galatians 3:28-29, we read, "There is neither Jew nor Greek, there is neither slave nor free, there is no male and female, for you are all one in Christ Jesus. And if you are Christ's, then you are Abraham's offspring, heirs according to promise" (cf. Rom 4:11-12, 16). Who, according to this verse, are Abraham's children? It is those who "are Christ's." If you are united to Christ, Israel's Messiah, then you are now part of the Israelite family. There is no longer Jew and Greek, but all are one in Christ. Galatians 6:15-16 reads, "Neither circumcision nor uncircumcision means anything; what counts is the new creation. Peace and mercy to all who follow this rule—to the Israel of God" (NIV). The rule of the new creation is that neither circumcision nor uncircumcision means anything. In other words, there are no longer distinctions based on ethnicity. Paul then wishes peace and mercy on all who follow the new creation rule, that is, the Israel of God. Based upon the immediate context and the letter as a whole, it is clear that Paul means new covenant Christians (the church) when he says "the Israel of God."

These verses cannot be dismissed. We are not through, though. Philippians 3:2-3 reads, "Look out for the dogs, look out for the evildoers, look out for those who mutilate the flesh. For we are the circumcision, who worship by the Spirit of God and glory in Christ Jesus and put no confidence in the flesh." Paul is clearly talking about the Judaizers—those Jews who would try to force Gentiles to live like Jews (see Gal 2:14). Christians are the true circumcision, those who worship by the Spirit, glory in Christ, and put no confidence in the flesh. Paul's "we" includes the Gentile Philippians. To say that new covenant Christians are the circumcision is to say that the church is Israel (by virtue of being united to the Messiah). John writes that the Word "came to his own and his own people did not receive him. But to all who did receive him, who believed in his name, he gave the right to become children of God" (John 1:12). The Jewish nation rejected her Messiah, but now all who receive him—Jew or Gentile—now are given the right to be the children of God, his covenant people. In Matthew, Jesus told the chief priests and Pharisees that "the kingdom of God will be taken away from you and given to a people producing its fruits" (Matt 21:43; cf. Matt 8:11-12; Rev 2:9, 3:9). Ethnicity no longer matters.[20]

Romans 2:28-29 is important as well: "For no one is a Jew who is merely one outwardly, nor is circumcision outward and physical. But a Jew is one inwardly, and circumcision is a matter of the heart, by the Spirit, not by the letter. His praise is not from man but from God." Being a Jew today has nothing to do with externals. A Jew is one inwardly, through the work of the Spirit. The Spirit circumcises the hearts of all who trust in Jesus, regardless of their ethnicity.

Ephesians 2 is a classic text on the unity of Jews and Gentiles in the new age. That passage reads:

> *Therefore remember that at one time you Gentiles in the flesh, called "the uncircumcision" by what is called the circumcision, which is made in the flesh by hands—remember that you were at that time separated from Christ, alienated from the commonwealth of Israel and strangers to the covenants of promise, having no hope and without God in the world. But now in Christ Jesus you who once were far off have been brought near by the blood of Christ. For he himself is our peace, who has made us both one and has broken down in his flesh the dividing wall of hostility by abolishing the law of commandments expressed in ordinances, that he might create in himself one new man in place of the two, so making peace, and might reconcile us both to God in one body through the cross, thereby killing the hostility. And he came and preached peace to you who were far off and peace to those who were near. For through him we both have access in one Spirit to*

the Father. So then you are no longer strangers and aliens, but you are fellow citizens with the saints and members of the household of God, built on the foundation of the apostles and prophets, Christ Jesus himself being the cornerstone, in whom the whole structure, being joined together, grows into a holy temple in the Lord. In him you also are being built together into a dwelling place for God by the Spirit.

Gentiles were at one time separated, alienated, strangers, but now, because of the cross, they have been brought near. Jesus has created the *one new humanity* out of the two. Now both Jews and Gentiles have access. They are both fellow citizens and are both members of the *same* household of God. Ephesians 3:6 says that Gentiles are now fellow heirs, members of the *same* body, and are now *both* partakers of the *promise* in Christ. It seems to me that only theological blinders can keep one from hearing the clarity of these verses.

The New Testament authors also apply many of Israel's titles to the church. The church is called God's saints, God's chosen people (Col 3:12), a holy priesthood (1 Pet 2:5), a chosen race, a royal priesthood, a holy nation, and a people for his own possession (1 Pet 2:9). The church is the eschatological Israel by virtue of her union with Israel's Messiah.[21]

Conclusion

Jesus Christ is the center of the universe. God has revealed himself over time, and the ultimate revelation of God is the Lord Jesus Christ. Now, everything is different. All of history must be seen in light of Israel's Messiah. New Covenant Theology takes 2 Corinthians 1:20 with utmost seriousness: "For all the promises of God find their Yes in him. That is why it is through him that we utter our Amen to God for his glory." I hope this little book has helped make that clear. There are many, many good and godly believers who hold to Covenant Theology and Dispensationalism. I myself have learned from many of them. As mentioned in the introduction, this is not a "primary issue" doctrine such as the Trinity, the deity of Christ, or the exclusivity of salvation in Christ, but it is important since it has a bearing on so many issues. Even if you are not fully convinced of New Covenant Theology, I hope and pray that you will strive to keep Christ central in all things. To him be the glory forever and ever! Amen.

SOLI DEO GLORIA!

Recommended Reading

Blomberg, Craig, "The Sabbath as Fulfilled in Christ" in *Perspectives on the Sabbath: 4 Views* ed. Christopher John Donato. Nashville: B&H Academic, 2011, 305-58. This is a 50 page chapter on the Sabbath. It is the best place to start in my opinion. Blomberg calls his view the "Fulfillment View."

Carson, D.A. *From Sabbath to Lord's Day.* Eugene, OR: Wipf and Stock Publishers, 1982. A collection of biblical, historical, and theological essays on the Sabbath. This is not easy reading, but is the standard on the Sabbath question in my opinion. A careful reading of this book will produce an advocate of New Covenant Theology.

The First London Confession of Faith 1646 Edition With An Appendix by Benjamin Cox. Belton, TX: Sovereign Grace Ministries, 2004. This confession has a distinct "new covenant" emphasis unlike the Second London Confession of 1689, which is basically a Baptist adaptation of the Westminster Confession of Faith.

Klassen, William. *Covenant and Community.* Grand Rapids: Eerdmans, 1968. This is a book about the hermeneutics of Anabaptist leader Pilgram Marpeck. He puts the canon together in the same way New Covenant Theology does.

Meyer, Jason. *The End of the Law.* Nashville: B&H Academic, 2009. This is basically a commentary on all the key texts dealing with Paul's view of the law. Technical, but clear and superb. Dr. Meyer doesn't use the New Covenant Theology label.

Moo, Douglas. "The Law of Christ as the Fulfillment of the Law of Moses: A Modified Lutheran View." In *Five Views on Law and Gospel.* Grand Rapids: Zondervan, 1996. I heard Moo call himself a New Covenant Theology guy in a lecture recently. Moo is very, very helpful. This essay is foundational!

_____. "The Law of Moses or the Law of Christ." In *Continuity and Discontinuity.* Wheaton, IL: Crossway, 1988. Another crucial chapter for the New Covenant Theology conversation.

Reisinger, John. *Abraham's Four Seeds.* Frederick, MD: New Covenant Media, 1998. This was the first piece of New Covenant Theology literature I read so it holds a special place in my heart and mind. John shows the weaknesses of both Covenant Theology and Dispensationalism by critically examining their presuppositions.

_____. *But I Say Unto You.* Frederick, MD: New Covenant Media, 2006. An exposition of Matthew 5 and its implications.

_____. *In Defense of Jesus, the New Lawgiver.* Frederick, MD: New Covenant Media: 2008. This is a careful response to Richard Barcellos' book *In Defense of the Decalogue: A Critique of New Covenant Theology.*

Schreiner, Thomas R. *40 Questions About Christians and Biblical Law.* Grand Rapids: Kregel, 2010. A wonderful, 230 page book on the essentials of law. Clear and accessible.

_____. *Galatians. ZECNT.* Grand Rapids: Zondervan, 2010. Dr. Schreiner is my favorite New Testament scholar. I really recommend everything he has written. Galatians is a very important book for New Covenant Theology, and letting Dr. Schreiner guide you through it will greatly benefit you.

Thielman, Frank. *The Law and the New Testament.* New York: A Herder and Herder Book, 1989. Dr. Thielman is a Presbyterian New Testament scholar, but he is a great exegete. This is a good little book on a complex question. I regularly call Thielman a New Covenant Theologian, but I am sure he would object. I am not sure how his exegesis in this book squares with the Westminster Confession.

White, A. Blake. *The Law of Christ: A Theological Proposal.* Frederick, MD: New Covenant Media, 2010. A study of new covenant ethics.

_____. *The Newness of the New Covenant*. Frederick, MD: New Covenant Media, 2008. All previous covenants find their fulfillment in the new covenant and it is radically *new*, not simply renewed.

Wells, Tom. *The Priority of Jesus Christ*. Frederick, MD: New Covenant Media, 2005. This book explains why "Christians must turn to Jesus first."

Wellum, Stephen J. "Baptism and the Relationship between the Covenants." In *Believer's Baptism: Sign of the New Covenant in Christ*. Edited by Thomas R. Schreiner and Shawn D. Wright. Nashville: B&H Academic, 2006, 97-161. This is a meaty chapter on the shortcomings of Covenant Theology, especially applied to baptism. This chapter is worth the price of the book.

Zaspel, Fred and Tom Wells. *New Covenant Theology*. Frederick, MD: New Covenant Media, 2002). This is a description, definition, and defense of New Covenant Theology. Very helpful.

Zens, Jon. "This is My Beloved Son, Hear Him!" *Searching Together* 25:1-3 (Summer-Winter 1997). A wonderful booklet on new covenant ethics and ecclesiology by one of the early New Covenant Theology thinkers.

Endnotes

1 It seems to me that amillennialism, historic premillennialism, and postmillennialism all have a seat at the New Covenant Theology table. Dispensational premillennialism obviously has a table of its own.

2 Ephesians 2:12; Romans 9:4; Galatians 4:24.

3 The Anabaptists were excellent on this point. See William Klassen, *Covenant and Community* (Grand Rapids: Eerdmans, 1968), 42, 44, 109, 110, 119, 123, 181; William Estep, *The Anabaptist Story*, 3rd ed. rev (Grand Rapids: Eerdmans,1996), 22, 42, 97, 126, 192, 194, 196, 226; *Anabaptism in Outline*, ed. William Klassen (Scottsdale, PA: 1981), 154, 156.

4 See Charles C. Ryrie, *Dispensationalism Today* (Chicago: Moody Publishers, 2007), 46-47. He writes that the distinction between the church and Israel is "the most basic theological test of whether or not a person is a dispensationalist," 46.

5 Christopher J.H. Wright, *Knowing Jesus Through the Old Testament* (Downers Grove, IL: IVP Academic, 1992), 71. G.K. Beale applies the same analogy in *The Temple and the Church's Mission* (Downers Grove, IL: IVP, 2004), 291. Thanks to Greg Van Court for pointing out to me that this analogy did not originate with Beale.

6 So Douglas J. Moo, "The Law of Christ as the Fulfillment of the Law of Moses: A Modified Lutheran View," in *Five Views on Law and Gospel* ed. Stanley N. Gundry, (Grand Rapids: Zondervan, 1999), 338; Thomas R. Schreiner, *Galatians* (Grand Rapids: Zondervan, 2010), 238, 248, 255, 397; N.T. Wright, *Paul* (Minneapolis: Fortress, 2009), 97.

7 See *The Westminster Confession of Faith* Chapter VII.

8 John Calvin, the father of the Reformed faith, directly contradicts Jeremiah here when he writes, "The covenant made with all the patriarchs is so much like ours in substance and reality that the two are actually one and the same," Institutes of the Christian Religion 2.10.2, ed. John T. McNeill, trans. Ford Lewis Battles, *Library of Christian*

Classics, vols. 20-21 (Philadelphia: Westminster, 1960; Reissued, Louisville, KY: Westminster John Knox Press, 2006), 429.

9 As Douglas Moo puts it, "With Christ as the climax of history, then, history can be divided into two 'eras,' or 'aeons,' each with its own founder—Adam and Christ, respectively—and each with its own ruling powers—sin, the law, flesh, and death on the one hand; righteousness, grace, the Spirit, and life on the other," in *Romans* NICNT (Grand Rapids: Eerdmans, 1996), 26. Similarly, Geerhardus Vos writes, "It is safe to assume that far more than all this counted the eschatological mold into which the Apostle's thought had been cast from is largely derived from its antithetical structure, as exhibited in the comprehensive antitheses of the First Adam and the Last Adam, sin and righteousness, the flesh and the Spirit, law and faith, and these are precisely the historic reflections of the one great transcendental antithesis between this world and the world-to-come," in *The Pauline Eschatology* (Phillipsburg, NJ: P&R, 1994), 60-61. Also see Jason Meyer, *The End of the Law* (Nashville: B&H Academic, 2009), 54-61.

10 Pilgram Marpeck, "Preface to the Explanation of the Testaments," in *The Writings of Pilgram Marpeck*, ed. William Klassen and Walter Klaassen (Eugene, OR: Wipf and Stock, 1999), 559.

[11] The ESV translates Hebrews 7:12 as "For when there is a change in the priesthood, there is necessarily a change in the law as well" (so also RSV and NRSV). The words for change (*metatithemenēs*), priesthood (*hierōsunes*) and law (*nomou*) are in the genitive case, not the dative case. A change *in the law* is a mistranslation. A change *of law* is accurate. Gary Long writes, "There is no reason to use the instrumental dative '*in*' to translate v. 12. Doing so gives leeway to understanding that the change in the priesthood and law was just a change in the *ceremonial* law with the *moral* law remaining, rather than a change in the whole law of Moses. Such understanding is based upon a three-fold division of Old Covenant administration of God's law into moral, ceremonial, and civil (judicial). But the Bible does not teach this threefold separation," in *Biblical Law and Ethics* (Frederick, MD: New Covenant Media, 2008), 54 note 58.

12 Richard Hays, "Christology and Ethics in Galatians: The Law of Christ," CBQ 49.1 (Jan 1987), 275.

13 David G. Horrell, *Solidarity and Difference* (New York: T & T Clark International, 2005), 230.

14 Hays, "Christology and Ethics in Galatians: The Law of Christ," 276, 286.

15 Horrell, *Solidarity and Difference*, 230.

16 I have modified the definitions of the law of Christ given by Douglas J. Moo in "The Law of Christ as the Fulfillment of the Law of Moses: A Modified Lutheran View," 343, 357, 361, 368-69 and Richard Longenecker in *Galatians* (Dallas: Word, 1990), 275-76.

17 D.A. Carson calls the old covenant "tribal" in *Showing the Spirit* (Grand Rapids: Baker Books, 1987), 151. I am indebted to him for this section.

18 James M. Hamilton, Jr., *God's Indwelling Presence* (Nashville: B&H Academic, 2006), 45.

19 N.T. Wright, *The New Testament and the People of God* (Minneapolis: Fortress, 1992), 402.

20 Dispensationalists appeal to Romans 11 to argue that ethnicity does still matter, and that God has a distinct future plan for ethnic Israel. A detailed examination of this chapter is outside the scope of this little book, but suffice it to say that I read the chapter differently. Paul seems exclusively concerned with the present situation, not the future. Note the time indicators: In verse 1, he asks if God has [currently] rejected his people and then points to himself as an illustration of the fact that God has not altogether rejected Israel. In verse 5, we read "So too at the *present* time there is a remnant" (emphasis mine). In verses 13-14, Paul writes, "Now I am speaking to you Gentiles. Inasmuch then as I am an apostle to the Gentiles, I magnify my [present] ministry in order somehow to make my fellow Jews jealous, and thus save some of them [today!]" (my additions). Isaiah 59:20 is quoted in Romans 11:26-27 and is often interpreted to refer to Christ's second coming, but this is a new covenant promise ("my covenant with them when I take away their sins"). The Isaiah passage is quoted to refer to "the Deliverer's" first coming, not his return. This passage applies to

Paul's current ministry setting, not a far off future event. Verses 30-32 confirm this: "For just as you were at one time disobedient to God but *now* have received mercy because of their disobedience, so they too have *now* been disobedient in order that by the mercy shown to you they also may *now* receive mercy. For God has consigned all to disobedience, that he may have mercy on all" (emphasis mine) If you are interested in pursuing this general line of interpretation of Romans 11 in more depth, see O. Palmer Robertson, "Is there a Distinctive Future for Ethnic Israel in Romans 11?," in *Perspectives on Evangelical Theology* edited by Kenneth S. Kantzer and Stanley N. Gundry (Grand Rapids: Baker Books, 1979), 209-227. Robertson has slightly modified his view of "all Israel" in *The Israel of God* (Phillipsburg, NJ: P&R, 2000). See also Ben L. Merkle, "Romans 11 and the Future of Ethnic Israel," JETS 43.4 (December 2000): 709-21; Lee Irons, "Paul's Theology of Israel's Future: A Non-Millennial Interpretation of Romans 11," Reformation and Revival 6:2 (1997): 101-24; Eckhard J. Schnabel, "Israel, the People of God, and the Nations," JETS 45.1 (March 2002): 35-57; N.T. Wright, "Christ, the Law and the People of God: the Problem of Romans 9-11," in *The Climax of the Covenant* (Minneapolis: Fortress, 1993), 231-57; Anthony Hoekema, *The Bible and the Future* (Grand Rapids: Eerdmans, 1979), 139-47. For those New Covenant Theologians who do see a future mass revival of "all" Israel, it is important to note that these Jews must trust in Christ and will be added to the church when converted, just like Gentiles.

[21] It must be pointed out again that the implications of this chapter result in a "believer's church." If the church consists of those who are united to Christ, then the church only consists of believers because one is united to Christ through faith. The eschatological Israel consists of Christ and his children. Jesus Christ has no grandchildren.

CPSIA information can be obtained
at www.ICGtesting.com
Printed in the USA
LVHW080548130620
657940LV00016BA/2514